Cradles in the Trees
The Story of Bird Nests

by Patricia Brennan Demuth

illustrated by Suzanne Barnes

Macmillan Publishing Company   New York
Maxwell Macmillan Canada   Toronto
Maxwell Macmillan International   New York   Oxford   Singapore   Sydney

Library of Congress Cataloging-in-Publication Data
Demuth, Patricia. Cradles in the trees : the story of bird nests / by Patricia Brennan Demuth ;
illustrated by Suzanne Barnes. — 1st ed.   p.   cm.   Summary: Describes the methods and
materials used by various birds to build their nests.   ISBN 0-02-728466-2   1. Birds—Nests—Juvenile
literature.   [1. Birds—Nests.]   I. Barnes, Suzanne, ill.   II. Title.   QL675.D46   1994
598.2′56′4—dc20   93-9114

For Aunt Mary V. Hermes, devotedly
—P. B. D.

For Suzanne R. Barnes, my mother,
who handed down to me her deep love of nature and her name
—S. B.

After the long, cold winter,
springtime comes.
The world leaps to life again.
New flowers peek out of the ground.
Green buds burst forth on the trees.
And skies are full of birds flying home.
All winter long, many birds stay
in warm places.
In the spring, they return home.
Some must travel a long, long way
to get back.
The little bobolink flies five thousand miles!

After their big trips, the birds
don't rest for long.
There is work to be done.
Soon the mothers will lay their eggs.
Baby birds will be born.
Where will the babies live?
They need safe, warm homes.
And so the job of building nests
must begin.

Barn Swallow

Bobolink

Chimney Swift

Robin

Hummingbird

Bald Eagle

Barn Swallow

Oriole

Flicker

Carolina Wren

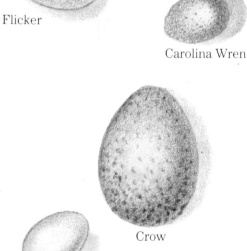

Crow

Meadowlark

Phoebe

Every bird makes a nest just like
the one its parents made.
How does it learn how?
No one ever teaches it.
It just knows.
Inside a bird's brain is a deep
knowing called instinct.
By instinct, every bird knows
just what to do.

Birds build their
nests in all kinds
of different places:

in the trees

on the ground

under bridges

inside the lids of old tin cans

on top of cliffs...

even inside chimneys!

The chimney swift glues its nest
right to the side of a chimney.
How can a bird get glue?
Its body makes it.
The glue looks like a brown liquid,
and it flows out of the bird's mouth
at nesting time,
right when it's needed.

Birds make nests out of all sorts of materials.
Whatever they need is found right
in their own neighborhoods.
Seabirds, for example, pick up pebbles
from the shore to make their nests.

Forest birds use parts of trees,
like leaves and tiny roots.

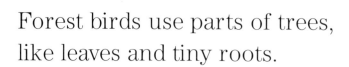

Field birds use grasses and weeds.

And city birds use string
or pieces of paper.

Take a look at the huge nest of the crow.
If you took it apart,
you might find cornstalks
  and pieces of rope,
  feathers,
  and cow manure!

How do birds put all the different pieces
of their nests together?
Some are weavers.
They weave together long grasses or
plant stems, using their beaks
like sewing needles.
When they're all done, their nests look like baskets.

Some birds use mud to stick the parts of
their nests together.
That's what the mother robin does.
Rain may wash away some of the mud.
She quickly goes out and gets more.

If you could watch the mother robin make her nest, what would you see?
First, you would see her carrying everything she needs to the tree.
She brings a pile of twigs and grasses, one by one.

When the pile gets high, she stamps
her feet on it.
That makes it flat.

She adds mud and stamps on that, too.

Then she presses against the pile with
her red breast.
The nest starts to get a nice round shape.

Next come the walls,
made just like the bottom.
When everything is done,
the mother robin sets herself down once more.
She twists and turns.
Soon her nest is shaped like a lovely
round bowl.

The mother robin builds the nest by herself.
But the father robin helps out in other ways.
He feeds the busy mother.
She can't take time to look for food herself.

He also keeps guard.
Other birds might want to build their nests
too close.

The male chases them away.
He makes scolding noises.
"Go find a different place," he chatters.
"This spot is already taken."

Mother birds are usually the ones who
build the nests.
But in a few cases, the father bird does the job.
The male woodpecker, for example,
makes a nest for his mate.
His beak is very sharp—sharp enough to
drill a hole into the wood of a tree.

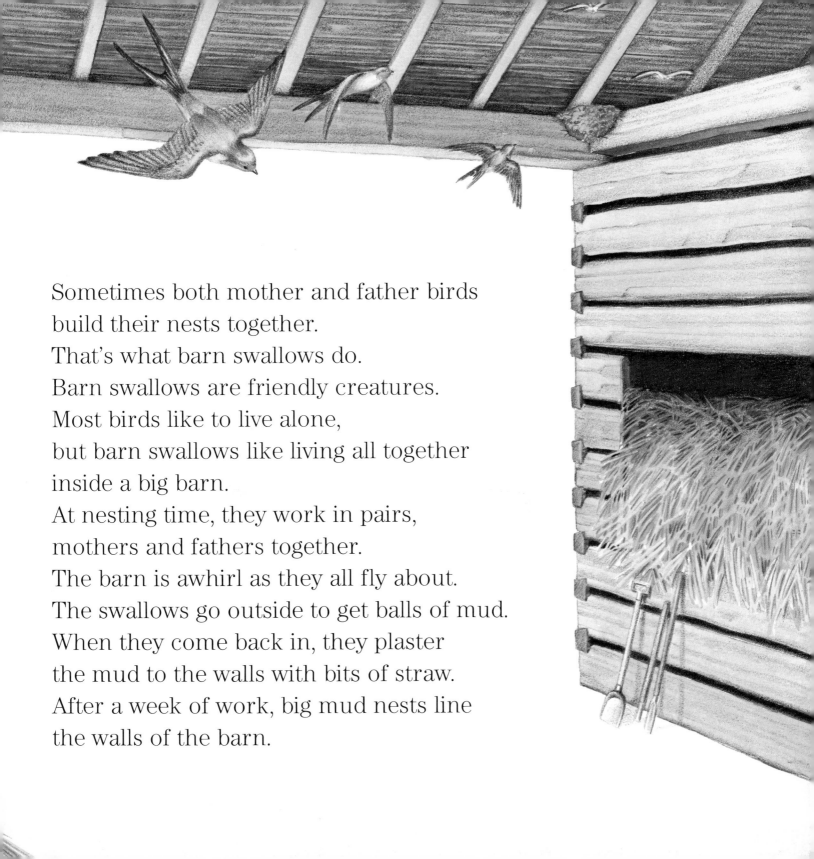

Sometimes both mother and father birds
build their nests together.
That's what barn swallows do.
Barn swallows are friendly creatures.
Most birds like to live alone,
but barn swallows like living all together
inside a big barn.
At nesting time, they work in pairs,
mothers and fathers together.
The barn is awhirl as they all fly about.
The swallows go outside to get balls of mud.
When they come back in, they plaster
the mud to the walls with bits of straw.
After a week of work, big mud nests line
the walls of the barn.

When a nest is all built,
birds usually add one more thing:
    a soft pillow for the bottom.
The softness keeps the eggs from cracking.
It also helps keep baby birds warm and cozy.

The barn swallows stuff their nests with chicken feathers.

Sawdust and wood chips pad the woodpecker's nest.

And fine grass makes a pillow for the robin's nest.

Birds are amazing architects.

Take the tiny hummingbird.
She is no bigger than a bumblebee.
Her nest is as small as a walnut shell.
Yet it is a perfectly woven little cup.
The outside is covered with green moss.
Sticky spiderwebs hold it on.

The nest of the Baltimore oriole
is a treasure, too.
It looks like a cradle with a long grass handle.
The cradle hangs from a tree branch.
When the wind blows,
it rocks the baby birds nestled inside.

Many people enjoy collecting nests.
Maybe you would, too.
There is just one important rule
to remember:
Take nests only in the fall or winter.
The birds are done with them then;
most birds will not use the same
nests again.

Start in the spring by laying out pieces of bright string or yarn.
Chances are, birds will pick them up and use them in their nests.
In the fall you may find your pieces are back again—as part of a bird's home!

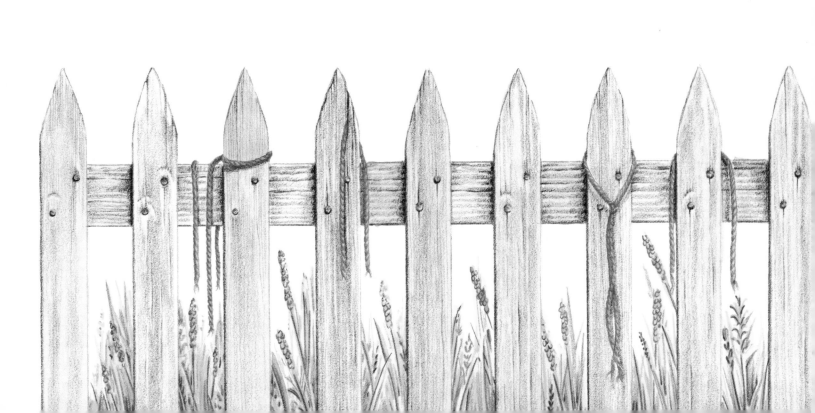

When the winter comes, look
at your nests.
Maybe you will think about the
hardworking birds who made them.
Those birds will probably be far away by then.
But next spring they will come back,
just like always.
And when they do, you will hear their chirps
and chitters fill the air.
And you will see them fill the trees once
more with new cradles for their young.